MYSTICISM, PSYCHOLOGY AND OEDIPUS

SMALL GEMS BY

Israel Regardie
and
J. Marvin Spiegelman, Ph.D.

Some Other Titles From New Falcon Publications

Aha! The Sevenfold Mystery of the Ineffable Love   –Aleister Crowley
Bio-Etheric Healing   –Trudy Lanitis
Undoing Yourself With Energized Meditation and Other Devices
Secrets of Western Tantra: The Sexuality of the Middle Path
Dogma Daze
   –Christopher S. Hyatt, Ph.D.
Rebels & Devils; The Psychology of Liberation
   –Edited by Christopher S. Hyatt, Ph.D.
Aleister Crowley's Illustrated Goetia
Taboo: Sex, Religion & Magick
Sex Magic, Tantra & Tarot: The Way of the Secret Lover
   –Christopher S. Hyatt, Ph.D., and Lon Milo DuQuette
Pacts With The Devil
Urban Voodoo: A Beginner's Guide to Afro-Caribbean Magic
   –Jason Black and Christopher S. Hyatt, Ph.D.
The Psychopath's Bible
   –Christopher S. Hyatt, Ph.D., and Jack Willis
Ask Baba Lon   –Lon Milo DuQuette
Aleister Crowley and the Treasure House of Images
   –J.F.C. Fuller, Aleister Crowley,
   Lon Milo DuQuette and Nancy Wasserman
Enochian World of Aleister Crowley
   –Lon Milo DuQuette and Aleister Crowley
Info-Psychology
Neuropolitique
The Game of Life
What Does WoMan Want?   –Timothy Leary, Ph.D.
Rebellion, Revolution and Religiousness   –Osho
Reichian Therapy: A Practical Guide for Home Use   –Dr. Jack Willis
Woman's Orgasm: A Guide to Sexual Satisfaction
   –Benjamin Graber, M.D., and Georgia Kline-Graber, R.N.
Shaping Formless Fire
Seizing Power
Taking Power   –Stephen Mace
The Illuminati Conspiracy: The Sapiens System –Donald Holmes, M.D.
An Insider's Guide to Robert Anton Wilson   –Eric Wagner
The Secret Inner Order Rituals of the Golden Dawn   –Pat Zalewski
Hinduism and Jungian Psychology
Sufism, Islam and Jungian Psychology   –J. Marvin Spiegelman, Ph.D.
Nonlocal Nature: The Eight Circuits of Consciousness
   –James A. Heffernan
on What is   –Ja Wallin

MYSTICISM, PSYCHOLOGY AND OEDIPUS

SMALL GEMS BY

Israel Regardie
and
J. Marvin Spiegelman, Ph.D.

NEW FALCON PUBLICATIONS
Los Angeles, California, U.S.A.

Copyright © 2021 New Falcon Publications

All rights reserved. No part of this book,
in part or in whole, may be reproduced, transmitted,
or utilized, in any form or by any means, electronic or mechanical,
including photocopying, recording, or by any information storage
and retrieval system, without permission in writing
from the publisher, except for brief quotations
in critical articles, books and reviews.

ISBN 13: 978-1-56184-502-6
ISBN 10: 1-561845026

New Falcon Publications First Edition 2021

The paper used in this publication meets the minimum requirements
of the American National Standard for Permanence of
Paper for Printed Library Materials Z39.48-1984

Printed in USA

NEW FALCON PUBLICATIONS

2046 Hillhurst Avenue
Los Angeles, CA 90027
www.newfalcon.com
email: info@newfalcon.com

CONTENTS

Introductory Note	i
CHAPTER 1	
Mysticism and Oedipus	1
By Israel Regardie	
CHAPTER 2	
Reflections on Regardie's Mysticism and Oedipus	45
By J. Marvin Spiegelman, Ph.D.	
CHAPTER 3	
Psychology and the Occult	67
By J. Marvin Spiegelman, Ph.D.	

Introductory Note

During Israel Regardie's life, he was a primary driving force behind western mysticism and magic. Colin Wilson, for example, wrote in 1982 that Regardie was:

> ...the last living representative of the great 'occult tradition' of the late 19th century, whose major names include Madame Blavatsky, W.B. Yeats, MacGregor Mathers, A.E. Waite, Aleister Crowley and Dion Fortune. Even in such distinguished company Regardie stands out as a figure of central importance.

Unlike the usual specialist in the twentieth century, Regardie was not limited to a small area of interest. He was a universal man, meaning he was involved personally and academically with all aspect of pyscho-spiritual development. Those who knew him personally can vouch for this. The many who did not, will have the opportunity to verify this for themselves, as his complete works gradually appear.

Before he died, Regardie gave many of his as yet unpublished writings to the Israel Regardie Foundation with permission to edit, expand and publish.

The present work is the first of these posthumous presentations. The centerpiece is the essay, written by Regardie in the late 1940s, called Mysticism and Oedipus. Chapter 2, by J. Marvin Spiegelman is a reflection on Regardie's essay.

Chapter 3 is an earlier paper of Spiegelman's on the relationship of psychology and the occult, which further compares and contrasts the viewpoints presented in Regardie's work, although it was written and published without awareness of the latter.

We are particularly desirous of deepening the Jungian and Reichian relation with magic and the occult (since these are our areas of expertise). The ultimate aim is a useful synthesis which will not claim exclusivity, nor be just another dogmatic school of "the way," but to sincerely deepen alternatives and assist the individual seeker in finding what is useful for him/her.

J. Marvin Spiegelman, Ph.dD.
Jungian Analyst

In honor of Israel Regardie we share this prayer that he was especially fond of:

"I am Osiris triumphant, even Osiris Onnophris, the justified. I am He who is clothed with the body of flesh, yet in whom is the Spirit of the great Gods. I am the Lord of Life, triumphant over death. He who partaketh with me shall arise with me. I am the manifestor in matter of Those whose abode is the invisible. I am purified. I stand upon the universe. I am its reconciler with the eternal Gods. I am the perfector of matter, and without me the Universe is not."

CHAPTER 1

MYSTICISM AND OEDIPUS

By Israel Regardie

Of all the problems confronting the earnest student of Mysticism–that is one who entertains the aspiration, and cherishes the ideal dearly beyond all others, of Divine Union–the most disconcerting is the glib and often hostile reiteration by the psychological amateur and professional alike that, "Mysticism simply has its origins in the Oedipus complex!"

Such an ethical injunction in Mabel Collin's *Light on the Path* as "Look for the warrior, and let him fight in thee…he is eternal and is sure," and some such phrases as "the worlds of rest eternal" in Blavatsky's *Voice of the Silence* are brusquely dismissed as indicative of little else but unconscious yearnings for the peace and security of the mother's womb. In the large majority of cases, needless to say, the individual making such a rash statement is wholly under the infantile impression that the empowerment of a conventional label fully explains the mysterious baggage to which the label is attached. (A later Regardie, would add that the findings of General Semantics are of central value in making such a discrimination. In fact, Regardie insisted that all serious students of Magic and Mysticism be grounded in the work of the Semantic schools, such as Korzybski or Vitvan. We would add our appreciation of Regardie's English style, reminiscent of that more leisurely and graceful period of the late 19th and early 20th century, to which he was related. Ed.)

Vox et praeterea nihil. No such folly is indulged in by the well-informed practising psychologist. Experience is such as to teach one that mysteries are not solved by so readily dismissing them with a phrase. And these are mysteries indeed.

The average student of occult philosophy is oft-times puzzled, nevertheless, by this apparently psychological explanation of his innermost desire, for he believes that the rationale, obscure and somewhat frightening, of the mother complex nowhere appears in his philosophical scheme. And since he is unable to reconcile the two, and in order, also, to protect his own feelings against further injury, he experiences the reckless inclination to reject the whole concatenation of observed and clinically verified data upon which a large part of the structure of modern psychology has reared itself. Rather than discard his mysticism, or even seek a clearer understanding of his beliefs, a wholesale rejection is resorted to. Likewise, the keen student of modern analytical methods and ideas, finding himself unable to discover in the works of accredited mystics and occult writers ideas parallel to his own scientific fact, flies to the other extreme. He becomes just as violent and extremist as the occult student, and discards the mystical contribution as having no intrinsic value–ambiguous phantasms of wish fulfillment and infantile regression.

(It is not uncommon for many modern-day psychologists and psychiatrists to regard an interest in mysticism, occultism, magic, and "offbeat" religions as a sign of schizophrenia and paranoia. In fact, one recent text-book on psychiatric diagnosis has a pathologic check list which includes the above as "signs" for the possibility that these disease patterns exist. It is of further interest to note that this reference book does not regard culturally accepted religions to be a sign of pathology, but instead regards them as adjustive and supportive to healthy ego-functioning. Apparently, health is associated with the religious patterns recognizable to the psychiatrist rather than intrinsic or scientifically based. In all fairness, of course, there is an empirical association between psychosis and occultism as well as an empirical association between vitamin deficiency and psychosis. Association–as all scientifically trained people are aware–does not imply cause and effect. Ed.).

Yet both these conventional attitudes are erroneous. The writer believes that the moderns, step by step, are approaching that psycho-spiritual edifice constructed by the ancient philosophers, and to which the name Mysticism, in its widest sense, may be given. To be quite truthful, however, even with the deepest erudition on cannot reproduce an *exact* comparison, inasmuch as even now science and psychology have far to go before catching up with the broad outlines of occult and magical psychology. The essential difference in all probability between the methods of occult and academic research is this. Mysticism has ever sought the universal, the broad generalization, whereas Psychology and Western Science as a whole have occupied themselves with the detailed and the particular. (Regardie is here concerned, we believe, with the problem of meaning. He is thinking of the pragmatic, technological attitude in academic circles very prevalent in the 40s, in contrast with search for meaning always found in the mystical path. Ed.). Yet it should be evident that the particulars *must* fit in with the universals. And the generalization must be so conceived as to include logically all the particulars–else one or the other is inaccurately stated. When attempting, therefore, the difficult task of comparison and reconciliation, a knowledge of the Qabalah is practically indispensable. The fundamental basis of the Qabalah–the so called Tree of Life (Etz Chaim) with its ten basic generalizations or *Sephiros*, amplified by a host of significant correspondences or associations of ideas, symbols and numbers–is the perfect medium not only of classification, but alike of comparison and synthesis.

Some mention must first of all be made of the Freudian dream-psychology since it is this scheme that has stressed and developed the root ideas of the father and mother complexes.

Briefly, the Freudian hypothesis postulates that underlying our normal waking consciousness functions a dynamic stream of instinctual energy, emotion and memory of infantile phantasy and desire, the sensuous dictates of which we, who live in an enclosed civilised society, find it necessary to repress. This clearly is understandable, since the community sets up a certain standard of ethics, a code of behaviour which is calculated (often in error) to protect its own social-biologic life from violation. Inasmuch as the vast majority of us refuse to attend to this dynamic urge to a more complete physical life, and since we do not consciously and honestly deal with the problem of the sublimation of crude energy, a brilliant and seductive pageant of sexual impulse, well-shrouded in archaic symbol, is presented to the individual during the hours of sleep in the fantastic adventure of dream.

The Freudian hypothesis also posits the ideas of repression–a purely unconscious and automatic with-holding from consciousness of ideas incompatible to every-day life. These ideas, thrust out of sight into the darkness of the Unconscious, group themselves according to the associative mechanism into constellations or complexes of ideas, dominated by certain themes, and charged very powerfully with emotion and psychic energy. Such constellations, as if overcharged with feeling, can irrupt themselves into consciousness by round-about routes, as it were, if the ego refuses consciously to deal with them. It is in the form of nervous and physical disorders that such irruptions take, and, in a minor degree, in the very upsetting phenomena of nightmares and bad-dreams. Sex and erotism, in their largest sense, are the theme motifs which dominate the constellations of ideas in the Unconscious.

On the one hand, many mystically-minded philosophers who should know better, unfortunately have denominated Freud and Freudian practitioners as "dirty-minded schoolboys." This opprobrium is absurd and distinctly unfair. It is by no means justified, since for one thing no fact however seemingly "dirty" must be ignored in scientific research. (Regardie stood alone among practitioners of the occult, in requiring himself and the field to confront matters of fact in science and the psyche, whether unpleasant or not. Ed.). Moreover, Freud was a pioneer in the realm of the mind, one of the first to introduce into the world of psychology the concepts of meaning, of purpose and motive. Therefore all honour is due him as a scientist of great ability and insight. On the other hand, while responsible for an immense amount of good in breaking down the molds of men's minds and in having helped to destroy sex taboos and false conventional notions of conduct, Freud has gyrated to the opposite pole. He has emphasized his hypothesis as of universal application and validity.

Whereas there is distinctly another type of individual whose background is not dominated by the sexual interest, consciously or unconsciously. (This would have been hard for us to believe in our college and early clinical years. In the course of many years of practice, however, a number of individuals have appeared in the consulting rooms who are, indeed, as Regardie states, not only not dominated by sexual interest, but sometimes even asexual or "neuter". The latter occurs, at times, without significant repression or pathology. This kind of individual, is quite different from the power-oriented personality that Regardie describes next. Ed.). His whole life is dominated by an urge to fulfill himself and to achieve, the will to power thrusting him forward from one achievement to another. Where this dynamic urge to self-fulfilment is thwarted, or, as in the case of some children, misconceived and a false style of life developed or a faulty conception set-up of their superiority goal, then here we have fertile ground for the manifestation of neurosis and physical disorder. (Regardie is here referring to the contribution of Alfred Adler on the power drive. He is also drawing upon the work of Jung, in his *Two Essays on Analytical Psychology* for example, who was the first to notice these two distinct types of approach to the psyche. Ed.).

In this connection one can only remind the partisans of both theories of the extraordinary clarity thrown on this problem by the diagrammatic Tree of Life, and the fundamentals of the doctrinal Qabalah. I must refer readers to the charts included both in my own works and that of Dion Fortune. (See *The Complete Golden Dawn System of Magic*, New Falcon Publications, 2020, and *The Mystical Qabalah*. Ernest Benn Limited, 1969. We also want to make specific mention of Regardie's creative contribution of placing the whole sex-power issue in the context of the Tree of Life. Ed.).

The Qabalah assumes that during sleep consciousness ceases to focus within the physical brain, and tends to return to the psyche. In the process of ascent it must of necessity pass through the Sephirah of *Yesod*, the Foundation. This sphere is described in the *Sepher ha Zohar* in such a manner as to indicate its sexual vital character thus pointing to an important correspondence with the Freudian idea of the Unconscious. The theory is that when a more or less profligate life has been consistently followed as the outcome of neurotic compulsion from repressed elements in the Unconscious, or one perhaps in which undue attention was given to sexual matters, the *Sephirah* of *Yesod* and its human equivalent the *Nephesch*, are thrown into a violent state of inequilibrium and disordered activity.

The opposites is likewise true, if there has been no sexual expression, and repression has played an over emphasized part in the individual's life. In such a case, the repressed material gathers terrific power to itself in the Unconscious,–and the result in both cases is a dream-like typified by a chaotic wealth of lurid symbolism, most of it of dubious connotation, preventing the consciousness returning as it were, to its own plane.

The sphere between *Yesod* and *Tipharas*, or that one level of the psyche, is called in

Qabalistic literature, the path of *Samech*. (Regardie holds that this letter means a "prop" or "tent-peg," that which holds or supports the house of our existence. The path is attributed to the zodiacal sign of Sagittarius. The symbol of Sagittarius is the Centaur, half-man and half-beast. This path leads from *Yesod* to *Tipharas*, the sphere of the Sun. The Taro card *Temperance*, would typify the Holy Guardian Angel to whom man aspires. The keynote of the astrological sign, the arrow pointing heavenwards, is Aspiration, and the sigil of the Sun and the gilt triangle over the heart of the Angel, all point to the object of aspiration, representing *Asar-Un-Nefer*, man made perfect.

As we have been informed, *Yesod*, the seat of automatic consciousness or the "home" of the Freudian unconscious, can be seen as a place were the majority of mankind lives. From this point of view, Freud's reasoning is valid–but only as far as *Yesod*. If the aspirant is capable of moving along the path of *Samech*, he may reach the plane of *Tiphareth*, where the dream content would not be full of "lurid symbolism." However, this is easier said then done, since it implies the removing of the girdle–the block at the diaphragmatic region, a Reichian contribution. One would also want to add here that Sri Ramakrishna would thoroughly agree with Freud, as noted above–most men/women live from the belly down. On the other hand, there are individuals who live from the head down to the diaphragm, those who live from the lowest chakra to the diaphragm, and those who function between *Ajna* [third eye] to *Tiphareth*. Hence at this point, we have three ways representative of the aspiration Godward. The fourth type is one who has removed the "girdle" or the belt, not through repression, and has opened *Tiphareth* through the path of *Samech*. This provides the meeting place where God and man meet. No longer do we have the image of the centaur, half-beast and half man, but instead, God-man or man-God. It is of great interest to note that the original Hebrew meaning of *Samech* is vibration or quivering. Thus the symbol of the snake, taken as wisdom in Kundalini yoga, gives us the clue of moving from our natural fixation at *Yesod*, to our higher aspiration at *Tiphareth*. Ed.)

Naturally the concept "higher" depends entirely upon the individual in whom it is dominant. The reaching for self-fulfilment, to manifest any higher quality is an unique and powerful experience.

"Our soul longs for God during the night, and our spirit seeks for God from the break of day. When man sleeps, his soul leaves him and ascends to the upper world. But not all the souls are able to come into the presence of the Heavenly King. When the soul leaves the body, she leaves behind her shadow [that is, the substantive aspect of the *Nephesch*–the astral body so-called] in order to keep life in the body while she rises from region to region, from step to step. During the ascent she comes in contact with impure spirits who lie in wait for her at the entrance to the upper regions. If the soul herself is pure, she rises above the power of these spirits and continues her upward flight. But if her tendency is to be impure, she is powerless to go on, remaining the whole night in the company of the powers of evil." (Bension's *Zohar*, p. 141.)

This particular rationale, however, does not apply universally, for "the souls of those who have not misused their bodies can rise without effort above the importunities of evil spirits." The Freudian hypothesis of a sexual dream interpretation, though having a very wide reference undoubtedly–for I should be the first to insist upon its applicability in many cases, and could bring forward many practical instances in support of it–is not universally valid. The fact is that many individuals, consciously or otherwise, have the various constituents of their being more or less equilibrated and integrated so that there is no *Nepheschic* disturbance to hinder them passing through the dream-state of *Yesod*. Then the ego enters a deep slumber and through the path of *Samech*, consciousness again centres in *Tipharas*–the proof being absolute refreshment and re-energisation upon waking. In passing it is of interest to note that *Tipharas* is the reconciliation of the preceding fourth and fifth *Sephiros* [male and female] and produces harmony and beauty. A quick look at the Tree of Life shows *Tipharas* as the centre of the whole Sephirothal system. (It is a common complaint amongst neurotics and individuals struggling with the problems of life, that they often awake feeling exhausted. Regardie's profound hypothesis that complete rest only comes when consciousness is centered in *Tipharas* is further validated from the stories and experiences of the enlightened Masters, who do with little or no sleep at all. This, of course, does not mean that everyone who awakens from sleep refreshed is enlightened or that those struggling with conflict are neurotic. As a matter of fact the editor has encountered such totally enlightened individuals, except on very rare occasions, and these only among individuals who are fortunate enough to be living a life style very different from that now experienced by most people in the world. In short, such serenity as suggested by Regardie's hypothesis is possible but hard to attain, not only inwardly, but in the face of the stresses of modern existence. Ed.).

With regard to the above quotation from the Zohar, it is imperative to remind the reader that "angels", "spirits', and "powers" of the practical Qabalah and Magic are, by one definition, "ideas" of varying degrees of power and significance which exist and function unperceived in the different regions of our subliminal consciousness. They are the autonomous constellations already referred to. Hence the evil spirits spoken of by the Zohar are, perhaps disturbing memories of the day stored in the pre-conscious zone of the psyche, memories which, together with repressed instinctual urges–the "powers of evil" so-called–tend to delay the passage of consciousness to a purer state or condition by the ghoulish symbols of sexuality which the *Ruach*, the conscious self, refuses or is unable to face in their stark reality. It is because I feel that the Qabalistic sages did know something of psychology, in their own way, and did understand of psychology, in their own way, and did understand so well the working of the human mind that I venture to re-state two or three of their theorems side by side with those of present-day savants in order that the subtleties of the Qabalah in both its philosophical and practical aspects may better be appreciated. Freud's hypothesis, then, is certainly true in a large proportion of mankind, as his own voluminous records testify. Any individual who is honest with himself is bound to be impressed with the truth of many of his contentions. But the theory cannot and does not apply to humanity as a whole without innumerable exceptions. (Perhaps a more satisfying statement would be that Freudian theory applies to all of us, in so far as we are functioning on the level of *Yesod*, but is not valid when we are operating from the higher levels. Ed.).

Having thus summarily disposed of Freud, let us turn our attention to the so-called Mother complex which will be considered as a general psychological theory shorn of all specific pathologies. (Regardie, once more, makes the creative leap beyond pathology–as if, he were himself moving from Yesod to Tiphareth in his thought. Ed.). Briefly, we may outline it in the following manner. Psychologists consider that before physical birth, the state of a baby must as nearly approach Nirvana in its feelings of peace, placidity and omnipotence as it is possible for any human to conceive. Its every need and wish is instantaneously supplied without the least effort on its part–without even any necessity to formulate the need in consciousness. There, in its mother's body, it is protected from external shock and danger. (Atlas, much research over the past two decades indicates that the fetus does react to external conditions as well as the emotional states of the mother. However, this does not obviate the point which Regardie is making. He is, in fact, speaking about the archetypal image, as Jung would call it, whose manifestation is subject to the flaws and vagaries of individual existence. Ed.). Little doubt can be entertained that the more or less sudden change from the intra-uterine life of complete tranquillity to the very different exterior world must come as a rude shock or awakening. (Aware physicians and psychologists are quite conscious of the transition state and have developed methods to ease the cross-over. Rank was the first analyst to have called attention to the importance of this transition, and Reich supplied more detailed theory and remedy for it. Ed.).

Life in the vale of tears commences as a sequence of effort, struggle and deprivation in an unknown and incomprehensible world. In the beginning of physical existence there is no essential difference between mother and child. One is part and parcel of the other. Even after birth, the mother exists as a constant and faithful source of gratification of the infant's hunger, and as the fulfilment of its every need. Psychically as well, a very close bond exists between the consciousness of the mother and infant so that there is but a little degree of differentiation between them. Whatever impinges upon the mother's psyche and whatever conflicts or pleasures are present in her, by necessity must play upon the growing infant's psyche.

For the rest of our lives, then, it may be said that we struggle against our human limitations, endeavouring to fulfil or attain to our infantile conception of undifferentiated ego which really implied effortless omnipotence, absolute peace and happiness. Hence the desire for a larger spiritual life, the aspiration to identify the individual human soul with a more comprehensive transcendental source of wisdom, bliss and spirituality–whether that be conceived of as God or the individual's own higher self–upon which in times of adversity one may unhesitatingly lean, has certain quite distinct parallels to the desire for the peace and comparative omnipotence which one enjoyed *in utero*. In each man, claims the psychologist, lurks the desire to possess or be possessed by his mother, for she is rest, fulfilment and safety. (Jung, very early on, emphasized the importance of this "symbiosis," or unconscious union of mother and child, in his *Symbols of Transformation*–the work which separated him from Freud but also provided the foundations of the archetypal psychology to which Regardie is here referring. It is also important to insert here that the first love of both male and female is mother, or the primary caretaker. Often this is forgotten. Thus all references to male in this context should include female, as well. This archetype of union transcends gender. Ed.). And so it is hardly to be wondered at that we manifest at times the tendency towards infantile regression, or harking back to that early period of our lives when mother meant so much and played such an important role in our development.

Second only in importance and significance to the Oedipus complex, is the so-called Father complex or imago. Although for convenience' sake father and mother imagos have been divided, it will be seen that they are in fact interdependent, the one being closely associated with the complementary feelings about the other. An understanding of this demands reference, so it is argued, to early tribal conditions in former stages of evolution. The primitive tribal unit then was held together by the tribal chief or patriarch, who was in a very real sense the head and owner of the tribal family. By common consent the patriarch possessed supreme rights over the members and property of the tribe, holding undisputed sway until such time as he was no longer able to maintain it by physical strength. It is easy to imagine that his authority was maintained only in the face of considerable resistance on the part of the stronger and growing members of the tribe. As the chief grew old and feeble, the power of his rule inevitably diminished, and thus grew stronger the criticism of those youths who wished to replace him. Eventually, either the patriarch died or was forcibly removed. Following a certain amount of quarrelling amongst the rival sons for the leadership, a new patriarch was installed in his stead. The two outstanding points which compel interest are first, the rivalry between the patriarch and the youthful competitors, and secondly, the rivalry amongst those desiring to become the patriarch. This conception of a recapitulation or unconscious rivalry adds to our knowledge and understanding of infantile and adolescent development.

We know from the purely physical point of view that all past evolutionary efforts are recapitulated and repeated very quickly the embryo. But the process of recapitulation does not stop with birth. It continues in the growing child who psychically lives through a state analogous to the condition of primitive man. Not only is the recapitulation process repeated on a physical plane by psychically also. On the one hand, preventing the complete enjoyment of the mother, or regression to an infantile state where one could wholly enjoy the mother, stands the father, possessed of knowledge and power or authority acquired through the status of his years.

On the other hand, are the feelings of criticism and frank disapproval felt by the son towards his father. As his own developing urge towards the fulfilment of his life becomes more pronounced so does the parental criticism. This manifestly has its basis in previous racial experience, the desire of the youth for the patriarchal post. In short, the father imago based upon this unconscious rivalry is firmly rooted in each of us. Like the Mother complex, as I hope to show, it is something greater and deeper than the mere disapproval of the actual father and love of the actual mother. It may be independent of them both and the reality of personal parental experience.

We have here two primordial images which, state the psychologists, determine the course of our ordinary intellectual life. The unconscious rivalry with and disapproval of the father, the innate urge demanding the imperative fulfilment of our needs and the attainment of relative omnipotence, and the desire for the apron strings of the mother who, we subconsciously feel, is still capable of gratifying our every wish. Between the mother and the fulfilment of this desire stands the father. These complexes of feeling, certainly not pleasant to face when unprepared in childhood or adolescence, are universally regarded with horror and loathing. When they do enter the realm of consciousness, instead of being examined and criticised, they are hastily thrust out and repressed forthwith. The repression of these impulses tends to imbed them the more deeply in the unconscious where, apart from any actual psychic disturbance of equilibrium, they modify and direct for instance our personal reactions to such worldly matters as politics, economics, religion, and domestic relationships.

What we are really to face here is the simple fact that one of the practical functions of the unconscious is the habit forming mechanism. Reactions of feeling and thought set up in childhood quite obviously develop after a very short while into habits. The reaction persists through the memory of the actual events or experiences resulting in the probability that the habit has been forgotten. These habit-reactions become consequently a part of ourselves, becoming deeply imbedded in the unconscious–the receptacle of "forgetfulness" as it were. Thus we mature with our unconscious loaded with a set of habit-reactions to external stimuli over which we have no control because we have forgotten how or why they have come into being. (Startling enough most human beings do not even know that these habit-patterns have come into being at all. This is why any mention of them may lead a person to hostility or withdrawal. It may be noted that Regardie combines the psychological interest in "habits" in the late 1940s, along with the Freudian image of the patriarchy. As I noted, it was a period when a number of attempts were made–largely unsuccessful–to combine these two modes of thinking. What is forgotten here is that both modes are metaphors, in fact, and that Freud's patriarchal imagery is just as close or distant from anthropological evidence as was the previously discussed image of the "ideal mother." What we are dealing with, we now know, and Regardie returns to, are archetypal motifs. Ed.). Amongst these habit-reactions are those relating to mother love and father hatred or rivalry. Because we are not conscious of them now in no way minimises their effectiveness as primitive forces active in the unconscious, producing compulsive behavior, moods and impulses, and stereotyped reactions.

Prior to turning from these psychological conceptions to a discussion of how to achieve a reconciliation with the esoteric philosophy, I want to consider in a slightly more extended fashion one more orthodox theory–that of recapitulation. By this term is understood that process by which an individual repeats a line of development representing a sum of previous racial experiences.

The best example which readily occurs to mind is that taking place in the development of the foetus. In the womb, it passes in a brief span of time through all those stages of evolution and development which have marked the biological progress of the human race in its forward surge. So that various animal and pre-human characteristics are indubitably present.

Recapitulation implies a speeding up of the time factor, so to speak, during which the experience of many thousands, perhaps millions, of years is repeated in the individual, both before and after birth. Anatomically and psychologically, the individual is recapitulating at different times the distilled essence of former racial experience. Thus the individual is himself but the apex of a vast pyramid, the base of which is formed by ancient history–racial and cosmic. But he truly becomes an individual, accomplishing the task of individuation, as he ceases to recapitulate the past, living exclusively in the present and acting in the light of a conscious adaptation of life.

It is this theory of recapitulation, I think, where must be sought a clue to a valuable comparison between occult philosophy and modern psychology. I believe that in this theory—also developed and expanded, though along different lines, by nearly all modern occult philosophers of any consequence" Blavatsky, Steiner, etc.,—will be found the means of at last providing a suitable explanation for the existence in the consciousness of civilized mankind of the mother-father imagos, and reconciling the ancient and modern systems of thought.

I deeply feel that modern psychology has committed a definite mistake in limiting its theory of recapitulation to racial experience alone, and this latter, in any event, is not wholly accurate in its present day recording. This perhaps is the root from which misunderstanding has grown. Occult philosophy not only fully recognizes, but expands in a highly comprehensive scheme, the idea of evolution—of cosmic and universal development which is recapitulated in the evolution and progress of the human being. "As above, so below" is an aphorism of the esoteric philosophy which, because of so frequent reiteration, sometimes loses force when we do not attend sufficiently closely to its implication. Man also, it is said, is the microcosm of the macrocosm—another well worn phrase, but one none the less worthy of constant repetition in spite of its familiarity. The *Sephiros* and the spiritual regions which are evolved metaphysically in the course of the manifestation of a cosmos are, by analogy, also represented and mirrored forth in the constitution of man. Whatever major processes are operating in the universe repeat or recapitulate themselves on a lesser scale and in a minor way in the psychology of the individual being. It is hardly necessary to enlarge upon occult theories of evolution. But in order to develop this reconciliation thesis, I propose mentioning the principal ideas involved in the Qabalistic emanation theory. (The present status of recapitulation theory, in both biology and psychology, is not as certain as its metaphorical use here. Ed.).

The mediaeval doctors of the Qabalah–more poets and mystics than philosophers–conceived first of all of Infinite Space, *Ain Soph*, as the spiritual source wherefrom all created things have issued, and to which at the close of the great cycle of manifestation, they will eventually be withdrawn. All things have their beginning, their period of growth, their goal of maturity and their fading away. And all these activities take place upon the initial and primary ground of infinitude.

On various of the Egyptian sacerdotal steles and papyri are vignettes and representations of the form of a woman whose body is so arched that her hands and feet, touching the world at different points, enclose within a limited area all things and all beings soever. This female form is the goddess Nuit. In the poetry of the ancient Egyptian cosmogony, she represents the omnipresence of space and infinity, and of her it is most picturesquely said that the Stars and the milk of the stars issue from her breasts. She corresponds in a unique way to the Qabalistic idea of the impersonal *Ain Soph*, from which the universe with its ten Sephiros or categories of creative thought evolved. Nuit is the cosmic mother, as it were, who gave birth from her own divine essence to the creative gods, to the stars and nebulae, to suns and planets, to angels, spirits and all sublunary creatures.

She is the mother of each one of us, although so far removed from our normal conceptions and speculative efforts as to be well-nigh incomprehensible and unknown to us, her children. I wonder whether it would be stretching philosophical probability too far to suggest that the first cosmic manifestations, the so-called supernal Dhyan Chochanic forces, issued from her interior life with as much reluctance as does a child from the womb of its mother? Consequently they bore within them an indelible impress of their spiritual origin, an innate yearning for the restoration of their primaeval Nirvana, the state of placidity and peaceful power, a craving which communicated itself to all the products of their ideation. Before manifestation they were part and parcel of omnipresence, of the celestial body of the mother, a unity in which no trace of imperfection marred the absolute serenity and ineffability of that life. Within the being of Nuit all was bliss and joy. But with the opening of the cycle of the active Day ensued duality–the great curse and teacher. And with separation, come deprivation and struggle and difficulty.

I do not wish to be so misunderstood as to countenance a return to anthropomorphic views, but I do feel that while it is a poetic one there is no uncertain authority for the employment of this interpretation. The suggestiveness of the idea is more appealing. From a philosophical or rational point of view I fully recognise that such an idea may seem childish and certainly naive, but that does not necessarily invalidate the essential *suggestiveness* of the concept. And that is all we require. For then our own intuitive processes will be restored into activity to divine whether such a view is with our without foundation. (At this point, Regardie returns to a symbolic mode of thinking, which does justice to both facts and imagery, without asserting the truth or falsehood of either. Ed.).

In point of fact, memory recalls a passage in the *Zohar* where, with gracious poetry and phantasy, it is described how the spirits of men were gathered before the throne of the Ancient of Ancients prior to being sent down to earth where they were to incarnate. In that heavenly condition on high, they expressed in no uncertain terms their unwillingness to be divided from their celestial sources of nourishment and sustenance, and to leave the divine womb. If this be assumed as a working hypothesis, that the gods or the divine cosmic forces which first issued from the infinite unmanifest at the early blush of the golden dawn, did so with a sort of unwillingness or reluctance–also corroborated by the dynamic tendency inhering in all forces to return to a state of inertia, that primal beings and coming into independent existence would likewise be impressed with that universal Oedipus complex, if so it may be called. The whole universe in all its manifold branches would be permeated with the inherent desire to return to the material source of life, for that alone can give peace, serenity and bliss. With the philosophic theory of recapitulation, this tendency would everywhere be repeated, though in a lesser degree. The cosmic endeavour to return, by evolution, to the primeval state of inertia would show forth in the unconscious desire of the child and every individual to return, as the Freudian psychologists put it, to the womb of its mother.

I am of course aware of instances where the primary spiritual instinct has become thwarted and then mixed up by the association with all sorts of animal impulses in which the perverse idea of incest plays a prominent role. But this properly belongs to psycho-analysis and its proper form of therapeutics with which just now I am not concerned. The complex as known to many of us is but a distortion, a perversion of a really divine urge–distorted because its underlying cosmic truth is unrecognised; perverted because it is repressed. It is the urge to seek not merely the physical womb, which is impossible and, were it in any way possible, of no moral or spiritual value for mankind. It is, rather, the urge to seek our divine heritage and place of birth along with the spiritual gifts of our earthly and human experience. (Regardie clearly leaves Freud's interpretation of the Oedipus complex at this point, and finds himself in between and Jungian views. Ed.).

I am well aware of the viewpoint that prevails in psychological circles. There it is held that primitive man, becoming aware of these primordial images within his own consciousness, projected them outwards upon the universe. He saw them not as factors implicit in his own psychic activity, but as forces moulding the universe and himself. His point of view is primarily to emphasise the objective, that is external, presence of these great generative forces, and then to assume that they are operative likewise within his own soul. Modern psychology calls this the projecting mechanism. It asserts, from its own seat anyway, an ignorance of cosmic processes, arguing that all we can know are the contents and activities of our own psyche. It is a return, as it were, to the subjective idealist view which asserts that the universe is the product of ideation.

But the fallacy is the assumption that it is man's own individual ideation which has produced all things. If it were asserted that all things sprang from or were created by the collective ideation or thought of the universe we would be nearer the truth. For man has not sprung, like Athena, full-armed from the hoary head of Zeus, but has a history of physical and spiritual evolution behind him. Also these primordial contents of consciousness have evolved from wider cosmic movements. These have recapitulated themselves, like most of the evolutionary efforts behind us, in our mind and bodies, and so have become integral parts of our world-view. (In short, Regardie is saying that the universe itself is evolving and gradually forming the categories of thought and image in the psyche itself. He transcends the philosophical duality between solipsism and objectivism by positing an evolutionary monism. Ed.).

There is another mode of consideration which may help to throw considerable amplification on the nature of these imagos, using the so-called Formula of Tetragrammaton, which figures a great deal in Qabalistic exegesis. It is conceived that from the first manifestation appearing within the infinity of *Ain Soph* flow forth in powerful waves of activity the four cosmic elements, four distinct surges of vitality, life and power.

There is another mode of consideration which may help to throw considerable amplification on the nature of these imagos, using the so-called Formula of Tetragammaton, which figures a great deal in Qabalistic exegesis. It is conceived that from the first manifestation appearing within the infinity of *Ain Soph* flow forth in powerful waves of activity the four cosmic elements, four distinct surges of vitality, life and power.

The first manifestation is considered to be a dimensionless point of concentrated Light, the first cause and the root from whose latent homogeneity both spirit and matter are subsequently differentiated. The four noumenal elements are Fire, Water, Air and Earth–not the terrestrial elements we normally cognize as such, but the soul, as it were, of all of these on a plane of metaphysical abstraction.

To each is attributed a letter of YHVH, the fundamental divine name of the Qabalah. In *The Book of Splendour*, further symbols of a most recondite and profound nature are associated with the letters and elements of Tetragrammaton. *Yod*, the element of Fire, is named the Father; *Heh primal*, is Water, and the Mother; *Vav*, Air, is the Son; the *final Heh*, Earth, is the Daughter. Thus the complex processes of the evolution of the universe, in all its heterogeneous aspects and multiform ramifications, are familiarly and eloquently conceived under the guise of a domestic relationship. For the union of the two primal elements, cosmic fire and water–or, as Blavatsky names elements, cosmic fire and water–or, as Blavatsky names them, cosmic ideation and root substance, the Father and Mother respectively–gives birth to lesser elements and other planes of substance, comprehended under the symbolism of the Son and Daughter, Air and Earth. From this association of four elements and their subsequent interaction proceed all manifested things and beings.

First we see the male, vigorous, cosmic force and power–the Father as it were of all life, alone, all-powerful, without rival or equal. It fructifies the passive female element in the universe, that receptive principle awaiting the germ of life that will make of her the pregnant mother, *Aimah* of the *Zohar*. From their union, motion is imparted to the vast masses of cosmic dust and thus the first nebulae are germinated. The process recapitulating itself within the nebula, we have neutral or *laya* centres being posited, to serve as the centres of globes of the planetary chains of particular solar systems. The entire impetus culminates as a propelling force in racial history, which is among other things represented today in every man's unconscious attitude towards, in short, not only his parents but everything else as well. Or rather, it culminates in the presence within the psyche of these archetypal images which, in the last resort, determines his life-attitude.

Inasmuch as that which proceeds universally has it counterpart within the human sphere, the larger cycles reproducing themselves in lesser cycles, the Qabalah postulates that these four elements of Tetragrammaton inhere likewise within the constitution of man. In fact, the Tetragrammaton formula is peculiarly useful as the type and symbol of man. As above, so below. Man in this particular scheme is a fourfold being crowned by the universal breath of the Spirit, the divine monad which transcends and directs the other principles, corresponding in the macrocosm to the Ancient of Days. There is Fire, man's spiritual soul of creative will, wisdom and authority— called the *Chiah*; and there is water, his divine soul on the passive side, including intuition, love and understanding, the *Neschamah*.

These two principles comprise with the Monad the higher Self. Air is the swift-flowing, subtle, volatile, fluidic power of the mind, the human ego, which is called the *Ruach*. And Earth represents the animal soul, the subconscious self which comprises the emotions, passions, instincts, and automatic impulses, the *Nephesch*. There is thus in man an active paternal principle and a passive maternal principle, the imagos or reflections within him of cosmic processes and developments. The Qabalists proceed yet further and believe that human progress consists in the union of the opposites. That is to say in the marriage of the Daughter with the Son, of the union of the subconscious self with the ego. In that union, wherein all conflicts and psychic problems of the personality are obliterated, harmonised and merged together–the Daughter principle is set upon the Mother's throne, and Son assumes the role of the Father. In this way, the animal soul submits itself as the handmaiden of the human soul, and the latter, discarding its complacency, worldly wisdom and false egoism, opens itself with love and devotion to the wisdom and intuitive rays of the Higher Self.

This classification has a certain validity in consciousness on practical grounds. I remember one dream produced by a patient of mind about a year ago. He dreamed that he was seated in a circular auditorium, at the far end of which was a lecturer. Try as he would, he could hear practically nothing of the address. Then and there entered two women. One of them was very indistinct and vague–almost ethereal; even her features were not recognisable. The other was a very definite, precise personality, clothes in black. Her dress was very scanty so that she appeared to the dreamer to be seductive. This latter girl seated herself by him, and the other one sat immediately in front of him so that he could not see the lecturer. Quite apart from the significance of the dream itself, the four people figuring in it could quite readily be interpreted along the lines of the Tetragrammaton inhering within the psyche. The lecturer represents *Yod*, the Father, wisdom and authority. The first indistinct woman is *Heh*, the Mother, love and intuition, without whom the address of the lecturer cannot be heard. The dreamer himself is *Vav*, the Son, and the black gowned girl is *Heh* final, the Daughter–the immediate problem. Not until her problem is solved, can the Son cope with the figure in front of him.

To look back a little now, the rivalry and intense jealousy in the primitive tribe as to who among the youths should succeed to the patriarchy was not really the ultimate traceable cause of the father imago. That is but a half-way house. The expression of an inner urge to power, this rivalry is based upon the dynamic impetus recapitulated from a former vast cosmic process. (At this point, Regardie spiritualizes Adler and the will to power, as he previously did Freud and the incest wish. Ed.). It propels man forward to claim his rightful place as the patriarch of his race, the creator of his family and the source of authority and wisdom to himself. What is required, as Jung as so well expressed it, is the domestication of the libido or *elan vital*, the harnessing of these great cosmic and spiritual forces which course as impulse in the mind and blood to the work and problems of conventional civilised life. (Regardie could not have known, as the time of writing this paper, of Jung's extensive elaboration of this "kinship libido" concept in his *Psychology of the Transference*, a work engaged in by Jung during World War II. It is, perhaps, worth noting, in this context, that Regardie always held Jung's theory in highest estimation, while preferring the methods of Reich in therapeutic treatment. Ed.).

Within the soul, latent, are tremendous powers which but seldom are given the opportunity to work openly. Only a fraction of them are manifested. And these, if ever they do succeed in penetrating the mind and heart of man, are usually prevented in their direct expression and turned aside from their proper course by centuries of false notions of convention, repression and ignorance of their true divine nature. Thus they manifest in numbers of cases as neuroses or worse. (The psychiatrist Lee Sannella, has elaborated this point in his book *Kundalini–Psychosis or Transcendence?* Ed.).

The psychopathologies of the imagos, however, cannot be dealt with just now. It is only the general conception which now claims my attention.

If he is to be biologically sound, man must continue in the cosmic tradition which inheres in the flesh of his body and within his spirit by virtue of the recapitulation process. By fulfilling his own self, achieving social adaptation and becoming the creator of his own family, and also by realising the paternal principles latent within his own psyche, he assumes the role of father and rids himself of the burden of the father fixation. It has been stated as psychologically axiomatic "that the goal of wish-fulfilment for the son is to become, biologically and psychologically, the father." To this, the Qabalist would add the word "spiritually" also, for as we have seen, without that the process psychologically axiomatic "that the goal of wish-fulfilment for the son is to become, biologically and psychologically, the father." To this, the Qabalist would add the word "spiritually" also, for as we have seen, without that the process is hardly completed.

In conclusion, we have found that because of certain cosmic activities and development there are within man what are called the father and mother imagos. The latter relates to the tendency on the part of the offspring to desire the tranquillity and power possessed not only in the physical womb, but in the unconscious Nirvana, that abiding city which preceded the cycle of manifestation. The other complex has reference to the indelible impress given to each constituent element of the created universe to become in its own turn and in its own right the creator. This is not only physically so, which is the least important factor–though one nevertheless not to be ignored–but is also psychologically and spiritually so. But this is meant that the human principle, which is active and spiritually creative, must be allowed to make itself manifest in the mind, heart and body; that the purpose of life and incarnation may be fulfilled.

So, in the future, when we have hurled at us the facetious relegation of mystical endeavour to queer complexes within the mind, we have no need to register vehement denials. What we must do is to answer "Agreed! But are you certain you understand the origin, scope and the real implication of this Oedipus complex?" And it will be found in most cases that in retracing its influence the psychological amateur will stop short at a certain point in racial and individual history and refuse to go any further. And it is here, as it is in almost every branch of philosophy and knowledge, that mysticism steps in with its ancient philosophy which has been developed and checked through countless aeons, to unravel the twisted thread of human development. It alone provides the key, possesses the true psychology which will unlock the fast closed door of mystery. Nevertheless it is gratifying to find academic and independent researches gradually and laboriously confirming the age-old conclusions of the divine wisdom. (Unfortunately, Regardie does not mention here, the specific academic researches to which he is referring. Sadly, the occult movement often tries to buttress itself with such vague references, a practice that Regardie, fortunately, rarely succumbs to. Ed.).

A vast amount of work remains for those of us who are students of this wisdom. We must not rest on our hard earned laurels, so to speak, and be content simply to accept the philosophy of the ancients on its own high merits. We owe it both to ourselves and to mankind to make sure that we understand our inestimable heritage, and to study the advancing efforts of modern scientists and researchers in every field of endeavor, so that it will be within our power gently to call to them from no great distance and point to our philosophic possession. Comparison, classification and synthesis, however, is urgently required. There is a great deal of work remaining yet to be performed in this direction and in the direction of self integration.

The integration to which Regardie was referring, seems to be a never-ending task. The integration of mysticism and the occult, along with psychology and science, is being continued by others. One such effort, is the publication of the present book. Ed.

J. Marvin Spiegelman, Ph.D.
Jungian Analyst
Los Angeles, California

CHAPTER 2

REFLECTIONS ON REGARDIE'S "MYSTICISM AND OEDIPUS"

By J. Marvin Spiegelman, Ph.D.

Regardie's graceful essay on "Mysticism and the Oedipus Complex" was written in the late 1940s, a time when Freudian psychology was in its heyday on the general psychological scene, but also faced heavy criticism in academic psychological quarters as being non-scientific. In those years, efforts at combining behaviorism–the darling of academic psychology–with psychoanalysis, were only indifferently successful. The seats of academic power were only indifferently successful. The seats of academic power were in the hands of the behaviorally-oriented scientists while the prestige in psychiatry and psychotherapy dwelt in the hands of medical psychoanalysis. Although C.G. Jung was appreciated in artistic and poetic circles and the first Institute bearing his name was founded in Zurich in 1948, both Jung and Adler were quite minor and thought of as outgrown aberrations.

I experienced the above situation first-hand, since I was awarded my bachelor and doctorate degrees in psychology at UCLA in 1948 and 1952, was trained clinically in the Veterans' Administration, and underwent a personal Jungian analysis during that period. While attempting to be proper and adapted by achieving good credentials, I felt quite the outsider spiritually and in professional interests.

I was mystically inclined in temperament, valued the art and literature, yet pursued a scientific psychology program which devalued both. I also embraced a clinical viewpoint–the Jungian– which was derogated.

Regardie must have felt even more the outsider than I did, since he was, first of all, a *magus*, a practitioner of the occult which many assume include the "black" arts. Not only was that interest one that was anathematized in both science and religion, he was also a chiropractor, a healing art denigrated by medicine as quackery. He was soon to become a Reichian therapist, a follower of a depth psychological school which was branded as more quackery and madness even by the analytic schools!

It is not easy to the target of negative judgements, even when there attacks are not personal but are aimed at the objects of one's deep interest and belief. Sometimes we are destined to embrace those ideas or movements we have rejected, perhaps by the law of *enantiodromia*, Heraclitus's formulation that all things tend to become or merge into their opposites. I can attest that was true in my case, since I abjured Jungian psychology when I was a callow undergraduate, yet ultimately became a Jungian Analyst, a view with which I have been identified for thirty-five years. As a graduate student, I also had contempt for what was called "chiropractic psychiatry" as well as the "quackery" of Wilhelm Reich. In my forties, I was to both bow to "chiropractic psychiatry," in the form of undergoing Reichian therapy with Regardie, and to appreciate the chiropractic approach in its own right. My suffering of the spirit led me to Jung and my suffering of the flesh led me to Reich and Regardie. I do not regret either.

The above example is meant to illustrate, at a personal level, how the "problem of opposites," as one can all this fundamental psychological principle, operates in someone's life when he is quite unconscious of the inner contradiction to his conscious ruling attitude. Indeed, the major work of every depth psychologist is to uncover these trends of the unconscious in a person and help him to reconcile these with the orientation of which he is aware. This is the empirical path toward resolving neurotic conflict and increasing conscious breadth and depth, to say nothing of advancing on the path toward wholeness and enlightenment–the desire of many in several of the camps.

The issue, then, is the "problem of the opposites," and Regardie's essay is a noteworthy contribution, at a particular time, toward the resolution of an apparent contradiction between a central concept in psychoanalysis and a honored longing of the soul, as found in mysticism. Regardie arrives at his reconciliation of these opposites, interestingly enough, by the use of Kabbalah, a branch of Jewish mysticism which itself was stimulated by Judaism's encounter with early Christianity and Hinduism. Hegel's philosophical idea of the conflict between thesis and antithesis, resolving itself in a new synthesis, finds its verification in cultural and spiritual growth, as well as in the psyche. And this principal has received its psychological development, in turn, in the work of C.G. Jung. We shall return to Jung's work in that area later, but first I wish to dwell a little on the struggle between science and religion, the larger opposites of Regardie's essay.

In the Renaissance, science finally emerged with a status and value of its own, after a fitful struggle with religious orthodoxy which, rightfully, found that here was an attitude and method which refused to submit to its world-view of faith. Science, on its part, starting with the reflections of Greek philosophers, the experiments of Egyptian embalmers, the advances in mathematical thought by the Arabs, and the general practical experience of the culture, burst forth with theory and technique which is still dazzling in its creativity and accomplishment. Its immediate forebears were in such proto-science as alchemy, in the view of the history of science.

Alchemy, however, as we now know, was not only an early attempt at chemistry, but was itself part of the long tradition of western magic and included itself among the spiritual disciplines, along with astrology, and geomancy. These, in turn, formed part of the pagan and gnostic underground of belief and experience only marginally tolerated by the Christian religion. As religious belief and experience only marginally tolerated by the Christian religion. As religious belief began to be questioned in the late middle ages, so then did the counterpole of hypothesis, experiment and empiricism emerge into consciousness. The early scientists, however, did not experience a conflict between their view and religion, just as the alchemists, by and large, did not, nor was there the modern contempt for the occult. Present astronomers are not fond of recalling, for example, that Kepler had just as much faith and expertise in astrology as he did in astronomy. Ultimately, however, the implicit conflict between the acceptance of tradition and belief on faith, versus the attitude of experiment and testing of truth, was bound to emerge.

It would appear, after several centuries, that this battle has been largely won by science, to the point where ideologies, such as Marxism, presumably based on the denial of religion and the embrace of empiricism, have won out in much of the world. The traditional religions, in the meantime, throughout the globe, have lost much of their spiritual command, although they have maintained a certain worldly power, as well as a lively capacity to resurge. Nowadays, though, we have religions which espouse science, and scholars of science who espouse religion. Science itself has often fallen into hands which are as narrow-minded as any religious authority of the past, and technology has more adherents and effect that any belief or "ism." We have discovered, too, that Marxism and other ideologies become "civic" religions.

In the twentieth century, even the soul has been subjected to scientific scrutiny. The result has been its reduction, in the work of Freud, or its denial, in the work of behaviorism. It is primarily in the work of Jung, it seems to me, that the opposites engendered in the struggle between these two ways of trying to apprehend "truth" have been reconciled. Jung has found, to use a variation of a statement of the gnostic Church Father Tertullian, that the soul is "naturally religious." He embraced a scientific way of both studying and appreciating this function, without being either reductive nor one-sidely doctrinaire.

When I taught a course in psychology and religion, some time ago, I asked the students to read several books, all of which shed light on the topic in question. These were Gerhard van der Leeuw's *Religion in Essence and Manifestation*[6] William James, Varieties of *Religious Experience*[3], Freud's *Future of an Illusion*[2], and Jung's *Psychology and Religion*[4]. Van de Leeuws's book, a phenomenology of religious behavior and experience, was a marvel of psychological and anthropological material amassed by a man who was a scientific, objective scholar, and also a "believer". James, too, tried to give his due to the religious experience, without losing his scientific attitude. Freud's book was clearly written by a man who had no religious experience, without losing his scientific attitude. Freud's book was clearly written by a man who had no religious experience at all. Only Jung's book, however, revealed the work of a man who was as knowledgeable and objective as van de Leeuw and James, but also had religious experiences vouchsafed few people and surely even rarer among scientists in the twentieth century.

Hence it happens that Regardie can refer to Jung in his essay and rely on his idea of the archetypal foundations in the psyche itself. This capacity of the psyche provides the underpinning to whatever religious experiences people can have. The historically profound difference between science and religion can be reconciled, as we see here. Jung shows us how, since both of these find their origin in the psyche and its nature.

If we return, now, to Regardie's attempt to come to terms with Freud's Oedipus Complex and its apparent reduction of the mystical longing for union with the divine, we find some interesting unexpressed (unknown?) dualities. The first of these lies in Regardie's reading of Freud's concept itself.

Regardie reads Freud's "longing for the mother" as a desire to merge with her, to attain the bliss of union and to be free of all care. His "return to the womb" is the equivalent of the Nirvana experience of the dissolution of all opposites. This is certainly a legitimate reading, but not the one that is customarily taken. Usually, this longing for the mother is seen simply as desire to possess her, personally, and sexually. The young boy wants to take the mother for himself, to own her, or dominate her and have her. To do so, he has to take her away from the Father, who is the one having possession of her. This is a grasping, taking, active stance, rather than the letting go, surrendering, passive stance implied by Regardie's reading.

Regardie's understanding is not surprising, in a way, since he experiences mysticism from the surrendering viewpoint. (It is of supreme interest to note that Regardie kept a picture of Ramakrishna next to his picture of Crowley, both of which he could view from his bed.). It is quite true that the mystical intention is toward union, and this is accomplished by a surrender to the divine. In another article I published some years ago (see

"*Psychology and the Occult*" in this book), I suggested that there was such a difference between the mystical attitude, which looked for relationship, love and surrender, contrasted with the magical attitude, which looked for effect, power and control. Of the two interpretations of the Oedipal desire, the mystical one implies surrender and love, and the magical position invokes active effort and power. We arrive, then, at another pair of opposites, even when considering the apparent unitary nature of a psychological complex.

The very word "complex" was coined by Jung, in the early days, to refer to a region of the psyche, partly unconscious and laden with emotions and ideas, in opposition to the conscious attitude. This came out of Jung's work with his association test and the evidence that slips, time delays, etc., were all a consequence of unconscious reactions which interfered with normal associations, and which occurred when a "complex"–as we term it now–was touched. Later on, it was found that every complex had an archetypal basis at its core or nucleus.

The analogy to the structure of the atom comes to mind here, with the archetypal opposites at the nucleus and the emotion-laden "electrons" of personal association, memory and image travelling about that center. The opposites in the atom also create the energy condition, as in the psyche.

Jung's view, even when considering the oedipus complex, turns out to be a broader, non-reductive one, compared with Freud's. For the latter, there is just one myth, so to speak, the universal oedipus complex, which implies battle with the father or tribal chief, and longing for the mother. For Jung, there are many myths, and even the incestuous complex is larger than the longing for the mother, since there is brother-sister incest, as well. Jung's interpretation, furthermore, is that incest desire is to be seen as the instinctual need for closeness, familiarity, intimacy and kinship, staying with the *endogamous* need of the soul. This is to be contrasted with *exogamy*, the soul's need to expand, to marry the stranger, to enlarge consciousness. These opposites, Jung shows, are both deep necessities of the psyche, and their interplay determines how much we reach out and turn inward. Indeed, although Jung does not say so, we can see that even these are the same as the ultimate pair of opposites of the psyche: turning inward versus turning outward, the basic temperamental opposites of introversion and extraversion. Both attitudes toward the psyche and the world are present in all of us, yet we tend to habituate the one or the other, until life and wholeness make us turn toward the "other" which has lain dormant in the unconscious.

We need to remember, after all, that Jung's type-theory was developed out of his attempt to understand his conflict with Freud and how he came to grief in that relationship. He was led to see that each apparent theoretical viewpoint was, in truth, also a statement of the psyche itself and at best expressed a kind of general typological view of the soul, of life, or the world. Thus Freud and Adler were also opposites, the one taking an extraverted attitude and also stressing love and relationship (Freud), and the other an introverted attitude and stressing power. Jung saw his own theory as accepting both and transcending them with a larger view, but he was under no illusion as to believe that his was somehow more "objective." He knew that his view, too, was conditioned by and expressive of his own psyche, and would have adherents only to the extent that other people's psyche resonated with his. One could discover universals, it is true (e.g. archetypes), but one could only transcend one's limitation of viewpoint by integrating the opposites that were to found within one's own psyche. Relatively was even more true of the psyche than it was of physics.

Jung's sense of the difference between Freud's theory, an extraverted one, and his, an introverted one, has been given further confirmation by a Jungian who has been a useful "anomaly," (self-defined), by being both an extravert and a very friendly to Freudians. This Jungian is Joseph Wheelwright of San Francisco and he found, through his own experience and the administration of the Gray-Wheelwright Type test, that by far the vast majority of Freudian Analysts are extraverted, with thinking and sensation as their preferred functions ([8] p.57). Jungians on the other hand, overwhelmingly tend to be introverted, and more likely to be intuitive or feeling types. In short, they are simply opposite to the Freudians. Since the United States is very much an extraverted and sensation-oriented country, it is not surprising that the Freudian view should be the more popular one, by and large. That Behaviorism, with its denial of the inner psyche altogether, should be even more acceptable tells us the extent to which our American extraversion is almost overwhelming. But all paths are ways to the divine, the old teachers inform us, and the truth is apprehended in many ways. We shall return to be behaviorism later on, but now I wish to compare what we have just discussed from a typological point of view with a look at the problem from another perspective, the attitude toward the feminine.

I want to preface this discussion by again giving a personal reference and reaction. For many years, almost every time I would read most Freudian literature, and even most articles appearing in the Kleinian/Freudian-influenced Jungian magazine *The Journal of Analytical Psychology*, I would get depressed. My attempts at understanding this reaction were singularly unsuccessful, however, and when I reported this phenomenon to the founder of the Journal, my friend, Michael Fordham, he opined that it was probably a good thing and the depressive reaction was designed to bring me down further into the body, the world and the earth. He was, no doubt, quite right. And his view was at least as helpful as my own Freudian interpretations of envy, inferiority feelings, etc. I was finally helped to understand all this more deeply, not long ago, by an article written by the Dutch Jungian from Amsterdam and Boston, Robert Bosnak.

In a brilliant article entitled "The Dirty Needle: Images of the Inferior Analyst,"[1] Bosnak takes Freud's "Dream of Irma's Injection,"– which is usually assumed to mark the beginning of modern dream analysis–as a kind of initial dream which often appears at the beginning of any analysis. Such dreams, Jung wrote, often "reveals to the doctor, in broad perspective, the whole program of the unconscious" (quoted in Bosnak, p. 105). Bosnak takes Freud's dream as an archetypal revelation of psychoanalysis itself, not only as an expression of Freud's psyche, but as a preview of the entire domain. The dream itself shows a startlingly clumsy and guilt-laden treatment of a woman patient, in which the doctors are unclean, inept, covertly sexual, venereal and incestuous–in short, inferior and "dirty."

Bosnak, using this "initial dream" as a paradigm, tells how he had always felt inferior and inadequate whenever psychic material was presented to him. Endlessly trying to learn and improve itself, he still felt this way and discovered that many senior colleagues similarly reacted even after decades of work. It then became clear to him that such inferior feelings in the process of analytic work are structural. They belong to the fundamental "experience of depth in the myth of psychoanalysis." His conclusion was that the inferiority complex is not just personal, but belongs to the foundations of the work. The images and feelings evoked are part and parcel of living and are particularly manifested in the role of the healer, since the effort to effect the psyche already confronts us with our abysmal inadequacy at the ego level.

I was greatly helped by Bosnak's article, as I wrote to him, since it explained why it was that I felt just such feelings as he describes, almost always in reading psychoanalytic (as opposed to Jungian) articles. I also had felt this inferiority feeling frequently as an analyst, but not so routinely. I would add to Bosnak's understanding some of the following reflections.

Freud's system is essentially a reductive, pessimistic psychology which is highly patriarchal in nature (e.g. penis envy, etc.), and is itself ambivalent about the feminine. The way the woman patient is treated in the dream shows the relative ineptness and potential destructiveness that adheres to such a view, even though there is a serious attempt to heal and help. I would take the dream as paradigmatic of that attitude, but it is far from the only point of view that one can have about the feminine or the soul.

It is interesting to compare this initial attitude toward the feminine, if one can continue to use such a metaphor, with Jung's work. We recall that Jung's doctoral dissertation, *On the Psychology and Pathology of So-Called Occult Phenomena*[5], was the study of his young cousin, who was a medium. In following the trance productions of this young girl, Jung gleaned what was to be his own attitude toward the feminine and the psyche, viewing the process as self-healing and teleological, producing symbols of growth and wholeness. He was "enlightened" by the process rather than clumsily trying to effect her. For him, then, the feminine was truly a "medium of the unconscious," although not literally a medium of the afterlife.

It is also interesting to note that his cousin developed a strong transference to Jung which he did not handle very well, not knowing, at the time, about such psychological events. So again we have intimations of incest (the cousin, in this case), and the challenge of the feminine, initially handled clumsily, but ultimately to become the soul-expanding work of a lifetime.

If we return, now, to Regardie's paper on Mysticism and the Oedipus Complex, we are further prepared to appreciate how his treatment of the feminine infuses the work in an equally enhancing rather than reductive way. Not only does he read the Oedipus complex from a loving/surrendering. nirvanic/union fashion, as we have already discussed, he also enhances and discriminates the condition in a brilliant fashion. He reconciles the "upper" and "lower" treatment of the sexual imagery in a way which offers justice to each. The complex is not reduced, it is "amplified" and expanded, as a Jungian might describe it, and he draws mightily not only from the work of Jung, but also from the formidable symbolic structure of Kabbalah itself.

In additional inadvertent (I think) tribute to the feminine, Regardie calls upon the image of the Goddess Nuit and locates her at the highest level of the Kabbalistic Tree itself. She becomes, in his reading, the carrier of the image of *Ain Soph*, Infinite Space, transcending all Sephiroth and issuing from the place where all creation arises and to which it eventually returns. It is an act of genius, in my opinion, to see the Egyptian Goddess Nuit, whose hands and feet, "touching the world at different points, enclose within a limited area all things and all beings soever."

Nuit, Regardie says,

> ...represents the omnipresence of space and infinity, and of her it is most picturesquely said that the Stars and the milk of the stars issue from her breasts. She corresponds in a unique way to the Qabalistic idea of the impersonal Ain Soph, from which the universe with its ten Sephiros or categories of creative thought evolved.

The genius involved here, I think, is the ability to link a very concrete and earthly image of the feminine as origin and nourisher, with the most abstract and transcending conception which may be seen by some as masculine but is hereby rendered in an androgynous manner, capable of expression in both forms. What a way to finally appreciate the "mother" and what a way to reconcile "above" and "below!" Would that such appreciations in word and image were able to equally effect this mundane world, both within us and in social life, as well. We are far from so integrating and appreciating the feminine within our collective souls and in the outer world. But as the century which began with Freud's *Interpretation of Dreams* and Jung's *Psychology and Pathology of So-Called Occult Phenonmena* draws to its close, we can see that the revolution of the soul is irrevocably on its way to a new age, in which the feminine will be equal as in Taoism and in the Kabbalah.

Since Regardie wrote this paper, the fortunes of the psychological schools have varied. Psychoanalysis lost its luster and power by the 1960s–when a religious attitude and need brought a strenuous challenge–but has recently regained attractiveness in the form of "Object Relations," when the world is, once again, more materialistic and power-oriented. In the meantime, Behaviorism has spawned a whole new therapeutics, in the form of Behavior Therapy. This modality made significant inroads into collective life since the treatment is briefer and cheaper, easier to sell to insurance companies, and is noteworthy more effective with such conditions as phobias and compulsions[7] (p. 426-427). Even newer therapies such as Neuro-linguistics and computer-assisted strategies have come over the horizon with similar social acceptance. Jungian psychology has grown also, during this time, less flashily, but significantly in prestige and numbers of analysts.

Whether our understanding has grown so significantly is not so certain. If variety of viewpoint, increase in numbers, multiplicity of little advances and reduction of authoritarianism can be taken as progress, then we have considerable. If certainly of knowledge or expansion of large theory becomes the criterion, then we have far less. But our time, the last part of the twentieth century, may be one of integration and reflection in the psychological fields. After all, the great figures of the century were all born well over one hundred years ago, and it surely takes us that long, culturally, to integrate what they presented to us.

Regardie's work here is one such attempt to integrate such psychological knowledge with the occult and mystical tradition. It is successful, in my opinion, and his use of the Kabbalistic Tree of Life as a metaphor for such further understanding is, I think, on the right track. More remains to be done to combine or compare the occult and mystical with the psychological, even though Jung has already been such a giant in the field. (A book along such lines, *The Sceptre of Power* is in preparation.)

References

1. Bosnak, Robert, "The Dirty Needle: Images of the Inferior Analyst," *Spring: A Journal of Archetypal Psychology and Jungian Thought*, 1984, pp. 105-115.

2. Freud, Sigmund, *Future of an Illusion*, (1927), Doubleday Anchor edition, Garden City, New York, 1957.

3. James, William, *The Varieties of Religious Experience*, Modern Library Edition, 1902.

4. Jung, C.G., *Psychology and Religion*, (1937), Collected Works, Vol. 11.

5. Jung, C.G., *Psychology and Pathology, of So-Called Occult Phenomena*, (1902), Collected Works, Vol. 1.

6. Leeuw, Gerhard van der, *Religion in Essence and Manifestation*, Allen and Unwin, London, 1938 (German original in 1933).

7. Miller, Neal E., "The Value of Behavioral Research on Animals," *American Psychologist*, (1985), Vol. 40, pp. 423-440.

8. Wheelwright, Joseph B., *Saint George and the Dandelion: 40 Years of Practice as a Jungian Analyst*, C.G. Jung Institute of San Francisco, 1982, 109 plus xiii pp.

CHAPTER 3

PSYCHOLOGY AND THE OCCULT*

By J. Marvin Spiegelman, Ph.D.

Three quarters of a century ago C.G. Jung wrote his doctoral dissertation *The Psychology and Pathology of So-Called Occult Phenomena*.[1] In that brilliant work, completed in the same year that Freud published his epoch-making *Interpretation of Dreams*, Jung sowed the seeds of many of his later ideas. We shall have to look at those ideas and their development in the course of our present investigation, but first I want to note that aside from Jung's contribution in this area, there has been very little advancement in understanding in this field. It is true that an increasing number of scientific bodies have recognized the existence of so-called occult phenomena since the patient work of J.B. Rhine[2] in the 1930s. And we all realize that the whole field has become widely and increasingly popular. But has there been an increase in theoretical understanding? We have laboratories in para-psychology which demonstrate–through experiment, Kirlian photography, and dream research–at such phenomena exist, but the explanations of such phenomena are hardly worthy of the name.

Why is that so? It has been suggested more than once[3] that the delay in acceptance of parapsychology by scientific circles is not because of lack of evidence. Indeed the statistical evidence amassed for extra-sensory perception is so enormous that were it in any more reasonable area of science it would have been embraced long ago. But there has been no theory to explain in a way that could be apprehended by the scientific world-view as it exists today. Not only would such acceptance upset the materialistic philosophical position of science (much of science has already abandoned the extreme positivism which is the father to such an attitude), but there seem to be no alternative answers either.

My answer to this question came after much puzzling and is so simple as to be suspect. I concluded that there has been no adequate theorizing or understanding of the occult field by the psychological field because the two *are* separate fields. Although they both examine the same general area, the psyche, each has its own theories. It would no more be proper to reduce the occult to psychology than to do the reverse. It would be better then, I think, to relate ourselves to these fields as "psychology *and* the occult." This implies that one could just as well study the occult of psychology–and perhaps with more enlightening results. For instance: what psychology, particularly academic psychology, keeps hidden (parapsychology) is central for occultism, and vice-versa (scientific criticism). We are likely then to advance our understanding of the occult and psychological fields by comparative methods, an approach which reduces neither to the other and maintains a certain respect for each.

Jung's interest in the occult and parapsychology[4] began when he was in medical school toward the end of the nineteenth century. Jung not only read widely in the area, but he did his own experiments. In 1988 and 1900, he organized regular seances with a medium who was his fifteen-year-old cousin. As well, he was having his own occult experiences at that time: a heavy walnut table in his home spontaneously split with a loud noise, and then a bread knife broke inexplicably into four pieces.[5]

Jung carried on the seances with the medium and published the results in his doctoral dissertation. He observed that the various voices or personalities which appeared to the medium were personifications of unconscious parts of her personality. He saw these, later on his development, as autonomous complexes, from which still later came the theory of archetypes. But at this early time Jung was impressed that the psyche was indeed not a unity but a multiplicity. Jung also noted that the flood of fantasies that came to the medium in her trances compensated the smallness and girlishness of her condition and that the rich flow of the material suggested an unconscious aiming at a greater personality, a larger whole than had existed theretofore. In particular, the chief figure who appeared in the trances revealed a more spiritual, aristocratic woman who was both an ideal for the medium and represented her future personality. Jung's understanding was validated some years later by the development of the medium into a stable and mature woman, out of the unstable young girl that she was.[6]

Jung noted that somnambulistic phenomena are frequent during puberty and suggested that these spirit states are attempts at character development. He saw them as:

> **...simply new character formations, or attempts of the future personality to break through, and that in consequence of special difficulties (unfavorable circumstances, psychopathic disposition of the nervous system, etc.) they get bound up with peculiar disturbances of consciousness. In view of the difficulties that oppose the future character, the somnambulisms sometimes have an eminently teleological significance, in that they give the individual, who would otherwise inevitably succumb, the means of victory (CW 1, pp. 136).**

Thus Jung brought forward a truly revolutionary understanding both of the psyche in its multiplicity, and the occult, in discovering the origin of spirits and voices. In fact, these partial personalities or "spirits" arise from the unconscious, and, as Jung's case showed, belonged to the medium herself.

This finding of Jung, strangely, is still not fully recognized in occult circles. Mediums I have met rarely realize or take up the fact, or even the possibly, that their voices represent parts of themselves, rather than entities from "the other side". Indeed one of the criticisms to be leveled at occult circles is that they fail to take up psychological self-criticism. It is too easy to attribute one's parapsychological experiences to other than an internal, personal basis, and thus miss the psychological development being aimed at the unconscious. The medium's lack of consciousness in this area, in my opinion, is what makes many of them either inflated or naive. In fairness, however, their lack of psychological criticism and the attribution of their unconscious personalities to the "other side" is not just illusion, but represents, perhaps, a true recognition that these complex entities are not merely personal but something more. We shall take up this question later. At this point we must merely note that the medium did, indeed, produce transpersonal material in the form of a mandala, a Gnostic system of the cosmos and its energies, which Jung recorded. After that, her material became shallow and banal.

At this point Jung caught her faking, and he abandoned the venture. The ending seems sad because I think the girl had fallen in love with Jung, and he seemed to have missed the personal connection with her. This is understandable for the young, scientific Jung, but gives us a hint as to what is ailing in the whole field of investigation of the occult. I see this as a lack of unification of the personal and the impersonal. Jung here lacked the knowledge and feeling to make a more adequate personal connection with the medium, which he would have done as a psychotherapist later on. He was too scientific and impersonal. And the medium failed to be aware that her voices were personal. She also was too "impersonal", but in a different way. Neither, of course, took up the problem of making a relationship with the voices or spirits, which the later Jung was to make the core of his life's work.

Jung's next theoretical paper on parapsychology and the occult appeared in 1919, when he spoke to the British Society for Psychical Research on "The Psychological Foundation of Belief in Spirits". In that paper, he explained spirits and other occult phenomena as unconscious autonomous complexes which are either projections or exteriorized projections. He said:

> **I for one am certainly convinced that they are exteriorizations. I have repeatedly observed that telepathic effects of unconscious complexes, and also a number of parapsychic phenomena. But in all this I see no proof whatever of the existence of real spirits, and until such proof is forthcoming, I must regard this whole territory as an appendix of psychology (CW 8, pp. 600).**

Jung continues the views he gleaned twenty years earlier, although he notes that these autonomous inner complexes can have an outer effect. (He notes this also, by the way, in his doctoral dissertation when he suggests that work with the ouija board can be happening so quickly, unconsciously, in the rapid reading of subliminal movements, that telepathy can be established.) Jung remains skeptical about "real spirits". The acceptance, however, that unconscious complexes can have an exterior effect on untouched objects (for example, in poltergeist phenomena) is already a huge step toward the occult. Does not magic mean the effect of one mental state upon another mental or physical one? If exterior effect is established, then one has moved a great distance toward the acceptance of the "reality" of occult phenomena. One **does not** thereby accept, however, that these spirits are separate entities.

Jung was to change his mind on this point when he published a revised form of this paper in 1948. By then he had formed his conception of the collective unconscious and archetypes, and thus had a new view of occult phenomena. He said:

After collecting psychological experiences from many people and many countries for fifty years, I no longer feel as certain as I did in 1919, when I wrote this sentence. To put it bluntly, I doubt whether an exclusively psychological approach can do justice to the phenomena in question. Not only the findings of parapsychology, but my own theoretical reflections, outlined in "On the Nature of the Psyche", have a led me to certain postulates which touch on the realm of nuclear physics and the conception of the space-time continuum. This opens up the whole question of the trans-psychic reality immediately underlying the psyche (CW 8, pp. 600 n15).

The theoretical reflections to which Jung referred have to do with his further work in the formulation of the archetypes and the collective unconscious. Jung had concluded that beyond the world of the psyche and its casual manifestations and relations in time and space there exists a trans-psychic reality (the collective unconscious), where both time and space are revitalized. At that level, there is a causality and space-time relativization parallel to the findings in physics. The archetypes are then conceived of as "psychoid", i.e., not exclusively psychic. Jung referred here to the archetype *per se*, not traditional archetypal images. This "psychoid archetype" is an unknowable factor which arranges both psychical and physical events in typical patterns, much as the axial system of a crystal preexists in the mother liquid of the crystal, although it has no material existence of its own. The psychoid archetype, therefore, is a structuring element, like the "pattern of behavior" in biology, that underlies typical situations in life such as birth, death, illness, change, love, and so on. The psychoid archetype lies behind both psyche and matter and expresses itself typically in synchronistic events. Jung understood synchronicity as an acausal principle which stands behind such event as telepathy, clairvoyance, etc.[7] Synchronistic events are connected through "meaning", a subjective factor, rather than cause and effect.

Jung's conception of synchronicity is a great advance in the appreciation of occult phenomena and their linkage with both depth psychology and natural science. However, the peculiar experience of causality in the occult field, the sense that the magician can "will" or "produce" changes, seems not to be reached by this conception. Synchronicity helps explain the subjective experience, so important in life, of "meaningful coincidence". It also provides a hypothesis for understanding divination in astrology, tarot, and the like. It does not explain the effects of magic in invoking forces, changing patterns through ritual, effecting healing or fulfilling desires.

So Jung's theory, while seemingly the best that psychology has to offer thus far, does not cover an understanding of the entire field. Jung had many parapsychological experiences in his life, and describes these beautifully in his memoirs, but he was reluctant to go further with them in a scientific sense. At this point, we shall shift our focus of interest from psychological theory of the occult to occult theory itself.[8]

Occult theories have various forms, ranging from the highly differentiated Kabbala, through the intricacies of Kundalini Yoga, the pictorial symbolism of Tarot, and of course, the many sub-theories involved in divination procedures such as astrology. Indeed, the Hermetic tradition in the occult suggests that behind every science there is an occult since which is more ancient, more complex and complete. For example, there is astrology for astronomy, alchemy for chemistry, and mystic psychology for psychology.

It is certainly true that all heretofore called "pseudosciences" are enormously rich in symbolism, but they do not constitute a set of principles as such, comparable to the laws of science. Much work would have to be done to translate into scientific formulations the basic principles of those fields. Fortunately, there are areas of the occult which have endeavored to do this. One of these, and traditionally the most ancient, is *The Kybalion*,[9] which enunciates a series of principles attributed to the most ancient Hermes Trismegistus of Egypt, said in legend to have lived in the earliest days of the oldest dynasties of Egypt, and to be the father of all the occult fields.[10] We shall examine the seven principles attributed to him which underlie all occult knowledge.

The first principles is that of *Mentalism*: "The All is Mind," says Kybalion. "The Universe is Mental." By this is meant that the Substantial Reality underlying all outward manifestation and appearance which we know as the material universe, matter, life and energy, is "Spirit," itself Unknowable and Undefinable, conceived as a universal, infinite, living mind. This suggests that the phenomenal world is a mental creation of "The All," is subject to the law of created things and exists in the mind of the All.

Now this principle seems to come dangerously close to the philosophical error called "solipsism," the view that only the subjective mind exists. Science and depth psychology generally operate with the phenomenological view: all that we can really know is our experience. But our experience also strongly suggests that there is a world of phenomena "out there" independent of our perception, and that we had better assume its existence, even if we know it only imperfectly.

The Mentalism principle, however, if examined in the context of Jung's views, may not be so naive and may fit in with our more expanded, modern understanding. As we know, Jung has suggested that the spirit-matter dichotomy can be resolved by considering the psychoid as a level of "spirit" beyond both psyche and matter, manifesting in each, perhaps synchronistically. There is a certain unknown and unknowable principle (similar to what occultism called "Mind") behind the archetypal images and experiences. Jung reports in his autobiography[11] on "leaving his body" when near death, and coming to a place where he saw himself meditating upon himself. He concluded that his existence was, indeed, a meditative imagination of a higher self. This is a parallel in image form to the occult principle of "Mind" and the All. Jung's experience, of course, like similar ones we each may have had, is not of sufficient scientific value to verify, but it is suggestive. The Hermetic position that "He who masters the mental nature of the Universe is advanced on the Path to Mastery," states the fundamental principle underlying the working of magic. The "psychoid level" as the basis of self-transformation in psychological works presents a similar notion.

The second principles of Hermes Trismegistus is *Correspondence*. "As above, so below; as below, so above," says *The Kybalion*. There is always a correspondence between the laws and phenomena of the various planes of Begin and Life. As geometry helps us measure astronomical distances as well as distances on earth, so can reason bridge intelligently from the known to the unknown.

The principle of Correspondence is elaborated in occult lore as the harmony among all the various planes: inorganic, plant, animal, human, spiritual. In psychological experience, we understand correspondence as synchronicity, i.e., where there is a meaningful connection among planes of events, physical and mental. We can find examples also in the parallel between alchemy and the psychology of the unconscious, where physical states are seen as projections of mental events and images. Whether Correspondence is totally true at the psychic level remains conjecture at this point for depth psychology, although this principle carries an aesthetic sense of order, which is part of what science also asks of its theories.

Vibration is the third principle. "Nothing rests, everything moves: everything vibrates." The different manifestations of matter, energy, mind, and even spirit, result from varying rates of vibration. We understand this readily in physics as the principle of frequency: sound, heat, light, electromagnetism, etc., represented by different rates of amplitude and rapidity of movement of waves, of frequency, or vibration. But the Vibration principle of occultism applies also to mental states of all types. Therefore, the presumed varying planes of the mind, from imagery to ever more subtle levels, also belong to this principle of frequency and vibration. This would imply that the mathematics of spectra, for example, might apply also in the mental area–something which is far from certain. Jung speculated that although matter is quantitative, psyche is qualitative. Psyche and matter may be considered as two aspects of the same thing, only one of which is measurable. The principle of Vibration is central for hermetic students who want to control their own vibrations as well as those of others. For them, the understanding of this principle is the "source of power."

We all know persons referring to each other's "vibrations," qualities given off and experienced as positive and negative by others. This seems more like an energy concept, better related to Wilhelm Reich's theories than Jung's, although Jung was the first to speak of psychic energy as a quantum back in the early days. Vibration, like Correspondence, is aesthetically pleasing, but as yet we do not have ways to assess the "mental" levels of vibration in terms of measurable energies. Here, however, the work of the experimentalists in Kirlian photography, in biofeedback, in aura research, in energy fields, may bring us closer to assessment. At the core, this principle would be more satisfactory to natural science.

The fourth principle of Hermes is *Polarity*: "Everything is Dual; everything has poles' everything has its pair of opposites; like and unlike are the same: opposites are identical in nature, but different in degree; extremes meet; all truths are but half-truths; all paradoxes may be reconciled."

This polarity principle is identical with Jung's first principle of the psyche, that of opposites. Love and hate, soft and loud, positive and negative, transform into each other, and, by the ancient Greek idea of enantiodromia, the opposites tend to go over into each other. This is true of psychic events, as many who have undergone extensive analysis can testify.

Occultists differ here from Jung, not in the principle, but in what is done with it. Occultists use the principle of Polarity by trying to change, for example, the vibrations of hate into the vibrations of love in one's own mind or those of others. This they do by meditating upon the desired pole. The Jungian approach, however, is to *relate* to the dark side rather than "think it away" by the opposite. In Jung's fundamental technique of active imagination one deals with a dark mood by descending into it, visualizing what it contains, and dialoguing with it, aiming at a synthesis with it, a union between conscious and unconscious. But the occult deals with Polarity by going away from one of the poles (**usually the 'dark' one**).

Rhythm is the fifth principle of *The Kybalion*. "Everything flows, out and in; everything has its tides; all things rise and fall; the pendulum-swing manifests in everything; the measure of the swing to right is the measure of the swing to the left; rhythm compensates."

This is again like the idea of enantodromia and is apparent in the events studied by physical sciences (oceanology, meteorology, etc.). It is apparent in the psyche as well. But as with the principle of Polarity, the difference between depth psychology and the occult lies in the use of the principle. Hermeticists apply what they call the principle of Neutralization to overcome the effects of Rhythm. They use formulas, rituals, and meditation to preclude the negative effects of Rhythm in order to achieve self-mastery. In this they are more like the conditioners and behavior-modifiers of psychology than like Jungians. This in itself is an example of opposites coming together. Who would imagine that 'scientific' behavior-modification and conditioning would be more in line with magic than is Jungian psychology?

The sixth principle, *Cause and Effect*, states: "Every Cause has its Effect; every Effect has its Cause; everything happens according to Law not recognized; there are many planes of causation, but nothing escapes the Law."

This principle, like the first one of *Mentalism*, sounds anachronistic, like nineteenth-century science. Does not science now speak in terms of probability, of statistical laws, of correlation, rather than cause-and-effect? Has not science–at the level of microphysics–given up cause-and-effect? It was on the basis of this transcendence that Jung and the Nobel-award-physicist, Pauli, came together in Jung's principle of synchronicity–that events can be connected by meaningful coincidence rather than cause-and-effect.

I think that the difference is both typological and a question of focus. By typological, I mean that the occultists and magicians are typically concerned with the will. By focus, I mean that the cause-and-effect principle may work in areas which are manageable, knowable, transparent, whereas the probability effect occurs just in those areas where the "law is not recognized," or too complex for understanding, or too multiple to be grasped. I think that there is no answer for the difference at this point, except to look at the conflict psychologically. By doing so, we may even be complying with the occult definition, which is to overcome Causation by going to a higher plane. This means that to escape cause-and-effect at one level, one goes to a higher mental level which rules the lower. This move is similar to "active imagination," the fantasy method of Jung, which is to overcome being possessed by archetypes or affects by increasing consciousness, a "transcendent function." We shall examine "active imagination" further after considering the seventh principle.

The principle of Gender is the seventh and last of Hermes Trismegistus. *The Kybalion* states that "everything has its Masculine and Feminine Principles; Gender manifests on all planes." This expression of cosmic sex, of male and female elements is everything, fully corresponds to the ideas of depth psychology. The occult understanding of gender is generally comparable with such Jungian fundamentals as Anima and Animus, and is visibly expressed in such systems of Kundalini Yoga, where each chakra shows the male character of form and structure and the female aspect of energy and power.

These are the seven basic *principles* of the occult. The several axioms which follow have to do with the *operations* of the occult. It is in these axioms that we see clearly the difference between the depth psychological approach, exemplified by Jung, which points toward consciousness and union, and the occult approach which aims at power and effect.

The Hermetic axioms that follow from the principles in *The Kybalion* state how the teachings are to be used, emphasizing active practice:

The possession of Knowledge, unless accompanied by a manifestation and expression in Action, is like the hoarding of precious metals–a vain and foolish thing. Knowledge, like Wealth, is intended for use. The Law of Use is Universal, and he who violates it suffers by reason of his conflict with natural forces.

1. "To change your mood or mental state–change your vibration." One does this by an effort of will, by fixing one's attention upon the more desirable state. One cultivates this capacity by increasing the power of focused attention.

2. "To destroy an undesirable rate of mental vibration, put into operation the principle of Polarity, and concentrate upon the opposite pole to that which you desire to suppress. Kill out the undesirable by changing its polarity." This axiom is a further variation of the preceding, through relating it to polarity. To sweep out darkness, let in light.

3. "Mind (as well as metals and elements) may be transmuted from state to state, degree to degree, condition to condition, pole to pole, vibration to vibration." This axiom elevates to a general level the preceding axioms, and suggest that time, patience, and practice will bring about increasing levels of mastery.

4. "Rhythm may be neutralized by an application of the Art of Polarization." Here we are told that the same methods as before can be applied to the flow of moods or states.

5. "Nothing escapes the Principle of Cause and Effect, but there are many Planes of Causation, and one may use the laws of the higher to overcome the laws of the lower." By this is meant that the hermeticist can rise above each principle and plane, by changing polarity, rhythm, cause, and vibration.

6. "True Hermetic Transformation is a Mental Art." Since the Universe is Mental, if one works on transforming mind, one can change the mental substance of the universe. In transforming one's self, one transforms all. In this, the final and highest axiom, we come close to the view of Jung also, although the way of proceeding seems different from the one he followed.

In contrast, let us here recall Jung's method of active imagination. In this technique the person relates to his unconscious through a continuing dialogue. This 'conversation' can be done with words, with art, or with movement. It begins with any mood, idea, affect, dream fragment, etc., that the psyche produces. The person then allows this content to personify, to speak or present itself, much as the medium experiences his "spirits." But then–and here the difference becomes clearer–the person begins an interchange with what manifests, bringing to bear all his own psychological knowledge, criticisms, questions, feelings. He is neither a mouthpiece for the "voices," nor a mere worshipping slave to the beings who emerge. Rather, he accepts the psychic reality of what he is dealing with, knows that much of what is produced is quite an autonomous part of himself–his shadow and contro-sexual complexes, for example– and that the rest is archetypal, that basic structure which clothes itself in the personal and particular. In this continuing dialogue, the aim is a mutual influence of conscious and unconscious, a healing of the split or separation that he has discovered in himself. The goal is more like that of the mystic, who has relationship with divine powers and seeks union with them.

Occultists, on the other hand, are interested not so much in relationship, as in power. They seek to train both fantasy and the will. Fantasy is trained by focusing upon given images–as in Tarot, or upon given rituals or prayers in magic. The implication is that if one focuses upon the given mantra, then predicted and known events will occur. In contrast with the open system of Jung, the occultist focuses upon training and conditioning his psyche; thus he is more like the behaviorist. The Jungian focuses upon relating to and understanding his psyche.

When we examine aims, we see a further difference, even an opposition. The Jungian aims at a differentiation of consciousness, individuation, and, perhaps, increasing the capacity to love. The occult aims at fulfilling his desires and gaining power. The former looks toward union with the inner world; the latter toward having an effect in both inner and outer worlds.

To a psychological observer, most occultists seems quite unconscious about themselves and quite inflated. They often speak rather pompously and know all the "laws" and "truth" about the psychic world. In a way, they are like walking archetypes of the seer, the magician, the old wise man or woman. They lack a critical sense and are quite unrelated.

To an occult observer, psychological types are pompously inflated with scientific or "objective" pretensions, are narrow-minded, and are insensitive to nuances of psychic energies and experiences.

To a third observer, both seem right. Inflation seems to be characteristic of those who work with the unconscious, whether in psychology or the occult. Indeed, dealing with that inflation, and the consequent deflation (negative inflation)–in short, the humanization of the archetypal level–constitutes the bulk of the work of the transformation process.

How then can the opposites of depth psychology and occultism come together? In a previous paper[12] I suggested that depth psychology was subjective science and that divination (a branch of the occult), subjective engineering. But we have found that the occult has its own science and theory, both in the broad sense as exemplified in *The Kybalion*, and in the individual areas such as Kabbala, Tarot, Kundalini, Astrology, etc. And so occultism cannot be exclusively a matter of engineering or practice.

Nonetheless, the distinction that I made earlier can still hold. Those areas of occult theory can gradually find their way into an improved depth psychological theory, much as the insights of engineers and agriculturists affect natural science theory. And this can be accomplished by making our *mediumistic personalities more psychologically aware, and our psychological personalities more mediumistic*.

It seems to me that we could achieve the needed validation of occult experiences partly by increasing the number of people who are capable of having such experiences. A trained scientist, for example, is necessary to examine the validity of experimental results. Most of us laymen simply accept them on faith, or on the basis of applied engineering. If many of us can be trained, or can train ourselves to be sensitive in the areas where mediumistic people are aware, then there will be validation by those qualified to observe. The reverse is also necessary. Mediumistic experiences should be treated, by those who have them, with psychological criticism, aimed at dialogue, differentiation, and integration of complexes. This could lead to greater consciousness, even if some might lose their abilities by such work.

Having made my proposal, I think it honest and necessary to state how this has turned out in my life. How does the coming together of the occult and psychology work for me? The answer is: not very well, yet. My slowness is the reason. And this slowness is precisely in the area of work with magic, with matter, and with the body.

I had worked carefully and religiously with Jung's technique of active imagination for about sixteen years. That work led to a break-through into another area of activity which I call "psycho-mythology."[13] a union of the opposites of fact and fiction, a merging of psychological fact with the fantasy that belongs with the archetypal, mythological level. This area, too, is a borderland between depth psychology and its methods, and the occult and its methods. It is neither purely individual, nor purely collective, but a blending of the two.

I seemed to have gone as far as I could with the method of Jung and came upon something else. More or less concomitantly, I came upon certain limits of the Jungian movement in other areas as well. These had to do with just the domain that magic is concerned with: matter and power. For me the Jungian method was limited in finally transforming those material basics, such as instincts, at a physiological level. I also found that the Jungian movements, collectively–like other analytic and therapeutic movements–had little consciousness of, nor had it transformed or come to terms with, the power question. These two areas–matter and body, power and the will–led me toward magic and the occult, and I have been slowly working in their territory for several years.

The work in which I am now interested rests upon the discoveries of *Wilhelm Reich*[14] concerning body armor. The melting of the rigidities and tensions shown in body armor is a long, slow process in itself. The ultimate result of this work, according to Reich, is the experience of the biological basis of psychic energy. It is this experience, I believe, that can provide a bridge between magical and psychological work.

A leading authority in the field of magic, Israel Regardie, has personally told me his conclusion after many years of work in both magic and psychotherapy, particularly Reichian therapy, that it is either futile or dangerous to work seriously with magic before one has had at least some psychotherapy and, preferably, has also reduced one's body armor by Reichian methods. Otherwise the energies released in magical work will merely cause mischief by being repressed into armor, or will be too much for the person to cope with.

I feel myself to be following Jung in a deeper sense, since it was he who carried forward the alchemists attempts to transform the soul until it could be united with a transformed body. Ultimately, we are told, comes the *unus mundus*, that one world where spirit and matter are truly united, not just with the person himself but also in the world of everyday life.

I would like to begin this final section on how psychology and the occult can come together by presenting a dream I had as I was working on this paper.

> I was cleaning a room I lived in, when I came upon a peculiar kind of instrument or a machine that I had presumably used before, but I was not aware that I had. This instrument seemed to switch on and off, individually and collectively, both the available lights in the room and also a whole bank of lights that I did not even know were there. I watched the machine do this for a time, and then used the machine myself. But then the machine suddenly vanished and worked autonomously. Now it showed its capacity to make objects appear and disappear. I was getting rather excited, but also wondering how I could let people know about this, or prove it. At that point, other people were in the room, and, as I saw a chair vanish, I called out to the people to see it. They did.
>
> Now, now only objects were able to appear and disappear, as had the lights, but also animals. Rats started to manifest and I grew alarmed at the danger of them proliferating. But then a strange, royal-looking cat appeared which could deal with the rats, and my anxiety was soothed.

I understood the dream as an experience of different levels of the autonomous psyche showing itself as being able to produce and effect consciousness (lights), the inorganic level (objects), and even the plane of the living (animals). I also understood my fear of the ravenous, destructively devouring, physiological level of the psyche (rats), and its needed balance in the appearance of the cat, who reminded me of the great Egyptian Goddess, Isis, who was mistress of magic.

When I told a colleague about his dream, she called my attention to a book called *Uri*, by a physician engaged in parapsychological research, Andrijia Puharich.[15] Uri is perhaps the most currently most famous and controversial psychic. He is a young Israeli who has performed telepathic, clairvoyant, and other unusual feats both on stage as magician and in controlled experiments as subject. This book tells of the experiences of Puharich and Uri, as well as others who observed not only changes brought about by Uri, but, supposedly, by "powers" above Uri who guided him. These powers not only turn on and off lights, make recordings on tape recorders, manifest animals such as the hawk, but also give messages about both past and future to Puharich and Uri, sometimes in the presence of others.

The peculiar thing for our present purposes is the similarity between what happens concretely and to several people at once in that book and what happened to me only in my dream. Lights, appearances, disappearances, even the animal (hawk, called Horus in the book; cat, called Isis, in my dream). It is as if the psyche is manifesting similar things at different levels of reality. I am puzzled by the similarity and am reflective about it. I conclude that the psyche is trying to communicate something to lots of people, and that the message seems to be garbled, or at least modified by the language, personality, and consciousness of the "receiver." For me the main message is that "powers" within or beyond man–need man!

Now, I do not consider myself mediumistic in the general sense, although I am quite attuned to the psyche by the nature of my work as a psychotherapist. Both Uri and Puharich are very different kinds of persons than I am. So, if I ask why this similarity between my "dream" and their apparent "reality." The answer that emerges is that there is an upsurge of this kind of magical material generally. For some people it is a living reality, concretely or psychically; for others only a potential; for still others, very far away. But it seems that the unconscious is striving very hard to affect us.

This was also the conclusion that Jung drew from his life-long experience with the unconscious, and from my own twenty-five years of work, I can only agree. It is both wonderful and psychologically curious–as well as humours–that these 'powers' take on technological forms, like robots, like robots or UFO's, or creatures from other planets, or voices and spirits, or angels and archangels, or figures that can be called archetypal images, depending upon the psyche through which these messages are filtered.

We can at best plod along, trying to develop both our mediumistic sensitivities and our psychological awareness so that whatever is going on collectively, either within us or outside us, will find us more adequate vessels to contain and cope with these energies or powers.

I realize that I have not taken up the important issues of scientific validation of occult experiences and the problems entailed therein, nor the interpretation of experiences such as Uri's and how they fit into psychological understanding. Nor have I discussed the mythology behind both the occult and psychology, which could deepen our understand.

I would not feel this paper to be complete, however, without presenting my own view about how the various antinomies and problems presented herein can be resolved. Briefly, I think that the two types of consciousness are differentiated polarities of the deep problem of opposites themselves. Whether one thinks psychologically, in the Jungian sense, or occultly, in the Hermetic sense, there is always some indication of incompleteness. One is either "spiritual" or "material," psychological-critical or naive-mediumistic. I have said earlier that one of the chief points of this paper was the assertion of the necessity for our psychological personalities to become more mediumistic and for the mediumistic side to become more psychological. Now I also want to suggest that we need a big jump in awareness: *a capacity to carry two or more different modes of consciousness simultaneously.* That is to say, we can become aware of and live in the mystical, pleromatic, occult level of consciousness and, *at the same time*, but fully cognizant of and live in the critical, interpretative level of consciousness. Furthermore, I think that our *everyday lives* could be as much a carrier of the mystical, occult, and synchronistic, as are the special numinous conditions.

What the alchemists thought of as the *unus mundus* and Jung explicated psychologically is a condition that is possible in everyday life, dependent upon our capacity to be aware in two or more modes simultaneously. The shift from one style of consciousness to another is one of the possible results of a successful integration of what Jung has taught us. Yet, this kind of simultaneous consciousness is less frequent than one would desire. I find myself injured and misunderstood most frequently by people who are, for example, confined to a personal, as opposed to an impersonal, mode of consciousness, or the reverse. However, it is possible to function simultaneously in both of these modes. In ordinary experience this would mean that people could think and feel at the same time, or note the facts of sensation and the intuitive possibilities therein. (This latter is a typological way of putting the opposition between the occult field and science.)

Whatever new facts and methods are developed in the occult and parapsychological field, whatever new drugs, techniques or meditative methods are offered, the solution to the fundamental problem of the union of spirit and matter, and of psyche and body, awaits our further capacity for both multiplicity of viewpoint and simultaneity of experience. It is in such conditions that the discrepancies between psychology and the occult are overcome.

*Reprinted from Spring, *An Annual of Archetypal Psychology and Jungian Thought*. Zurich, 1976.

Many thanks are given to James Hillman, Ph.D. for his kind permission to reprint this article.

Note: "pp" in this reprint stands for paragraph and not pages.

References

1. C.G. Jung, "On the Psychology and Pathology of So-called Occult Phenomena" (1902), CW1.

2. J.B. Rhine, *The Reach of the Mind* (London: Penguin, 1948).

3. E.g., A. Jaffe (below) quoting *Encyclopedia Britannica*, 1961, .

4. Aniela Jaffe, *From the Life and Work of C.G. Jung* (N.Y.: Harper & Row, 1971).

5. C.G. Jung, (with A. Jaffe), *Memories, Dreams, Reflections*, transl. R. & C. Winstion (N.Y.: Pantheon 1961), p. 105.

6. See below, pp. 123ff for reference to a biography of the medium of Stefanie Zumstien-Preiswerk.

7. C.G. Jung, "Synchronicity: An Acausal Connecting Principle" (1952), CW 8.

8. For particularly good introductions to the occult field as magic, and to occult theory, see W.E. Butler, *The Magician: His Training and Work* (N. Hollywood: Wilshire Book Co., 1972) and Israel Regardie, *The Tree of Life: A Study in Magic* (N.Y.: Samuel Weiser, 1969).

9. Anonymous, *The Kybalion, Hermetic Philosophy* (Chicago: Yogi Publication Society, 1936).

10. For a more scholarly examination of this material, see the classic, three-volume work of G.R.S. Mead, *Thrice–Greatest Hermes: Studies in Hellenistic Philosophy and Gnosis* (London: Watkins, 1964).

11. Jung, *Memories, Dreams, Reflections*, op. cit., pp. 289ff.

12. J.M. Spiegleman, "Mythical and Scientific Basis of Divination," 1971, unpublished.

13. J.M. Spiegleman, *The Tree: Tales in Psychomythology* (Phoenix: Falcon Press, 1982).

14. Wilhelm Reich, *Character Analysis*, 3rd ed. (N.Y.: Orgone Institute press, 1949).

15. Andrjia Puharich, *Uri: A Journal of the Mystery of Uri Geller* (N.Y.: Doubleday Anchor, 1974).

NEW FALCON PUBLICATIONS

*Publisher of Controversial Books and CDs
Invites you to visit our website*

www.newfalcon.com

- Browse the online catalog of all our great titles, including books by Israel Regardie, Christopher S. Hyatt, Robert Anton Wilson, Aleister Crowley, Timothy Leary, Osho, Lon Milo DuQuette and many more.
- Get special discounts
- Order our titles through our secure online server
- Find products not available anywhere else
    - One of a kind and limited availability products
    - Special packages
    - Special pricing
- And much, more more